Verschoyle Surname

Ireland: 1600s to 1900s

From Ireland Church Records of Baptism, Marriage and Death

Comprised of Roman Catholic and Church of Ireland Records

From Counties Carlow, Cork, Kerry and Dublin City

Compiled by **Donovan Hurst**

December 1, 2011

Dedication

This work is dedicated to all of those that came before us and shaped our lives to make us the people that we are today.

Table of Contents

Introduction

This is a compilation of individuals who have the surname of Verschoyle that lived in the country of Ireland from the 1600s to the 1900s. I have placed each entry into one of four categories: Families, Individual Births/Baptisms, Individual Burials, and Individual Marriages. If a marriage entry primarily concerns an Individual Verschoyle who is female, then I have placed that entry under the category of Individual Marriages. If a marriage entry primarily concerns an Individual Verschoyle who is male, then I have placed that entry under the category of Families. Images of many of these listings are available at http://churchrecords.irishgenealogy.ie/churchrecords/.

To help guide the reader of this work, the format of this book is as follows:

- **Main Family Entry (Husband and Wife) (Father and Mother)**

  o **Child of Main Family Entry, including Spouse(s) when available**

    ▪ Grandchild of Main Family Entry, including Spouse(s) when available

    • Great-Grandchild of Main Family Entry, including Spouse(s) when available

(**Bolded Text**) following any entry includes any additional information such as Residence(s), Occupation(s), Signature(s), etc. when available.

Hurst

Some of the fonts used in this work symbolizes Celtic writing. The traditional letters, numbers, and punctuation marks and their Celtic counterparts are as follows:

Traditional Letters (Uppercase & Lowercase)

A a B b C c D d E f G g H h I i J j K k L l M m N n O o P p Q q R r S s T t U u V v W w X x Y y Z z

Celtic Letters (Uppercase & Lowercase)

A a B b C c D ð E e F ꝼ G g H h I í J j K k L l M m

N n O o P p Q q R ʀ S s T t U u V ʋ W ω X x Y ꝡ Z z

Traditional Numbers

1 2 3 4 5 6 7 8 9 10

Celtic Numbers

1 2 3 4 5 6 7 8 9 10

Traditional Punctuation

. , : ' " & - ( )

Celtic Punctuation

. , : ' " & - ( )

Parish Churches

Dublin (Church of Ireland)

Arbour Hill Barracks Parish, Leeson Park Parish, Rathcoole Parish, Richmond Barracks Parish, St. Anne Parish, St. Audoen Parish, St. Catherine Parish, St. James Parish, St. Luke Parish, St. Mark Parish, St. Paul Parish, St. Peter Parish, St. Stephen Parish, St. Werburgh Parish, and Taney Parish.

Dublin (Roman Catholic or RC)

Harrington Street Parish, St. Catherine Parish, St. James Parish, St. Mary, Pro Cathedral Parish, St. Michan Parish, and St. Nicholas Parish.

Families

- Benjamin Verschoyle & Elizabeth Unknown

  o Edward Verschoyle – bapt. 22 Sep 1799 (Baptism, **St. Catherine Parish**)

Benjamin Verschoyle (father):

Residence - Irwin Street - September 1799

- Benjamin Verschoyle & Jane Hanlon

  o Susanna Bridget Josephine Verschoyle, b. 29 Dec 1856, bapt. 1 Jan 1857 (Baptism, **St. James Parish**

  (RC)) & Joseph Matthew Reidy – 22 Nov 1881 (Marriage, **Harrington Street Parish** (RC))

  ▪ Mary Josephine Reidy – b. 6 Apr 1884, bapt. 14 Apr 1884 (Baptism, **St. Michan Parish** (RC))

Susanna Verschoyle (daughter):

Residence - Ropers Rest - November 22, 1881

Joseph Matthew Reidy, son of James Reidy & Helen McAuliffe (son-in-law):

Residence - Angel Hotel - November 22, 1881

26 Palmerstown Place - April 14, 1884

  o Mary Verschoyle – b. 13 Aug 1858, bapt. 16 Aug 1858 (Baptism, **St. James Parish** (RC))

  o Thomas Patrick Verschoyle – b. 26 Feb 1860, bapt. 3 Mar 1860 (Baptism, **St. James Parish** (RC))

  o Jane Verschoyle – b. 28 Aug 1861, bapt. 9 Sep 1861 (Baptism, **St. James Parish** (RC))

  o James Verschoyle – b. 6 Jul 1870, bapt. 8 Jul 1870 (Baptism, **Harrington Street Parish** (RC))

  o Anne Virginia Frances Verschoyle – b. 8 Sep 1872, bapt. 17 Sep 1872 (Baptism, **Harrington Street**

  Parish (RC))

  o Josephine Mary Verschoyle – b. 8 Oct 1877, bapt. 11 Oct 1877 (Baptism, **Harrington Street**

  Parish (RC))

Hurst

Benjamin Verschoyle (father):

Residence - 16 Watling Street - January 1, 1857

August 16, 1858

March 3, 1860

September 9, 1861

Ropers Rest - July 8, 1870

October 11, 1877

Greenville Avenue - September 17, 1872

- Benjamin Verschoyle & Mary Unknown

  o Mary Verschoyle – bapt. 3 Aug 1796 (Baptism, **St. Catherine Parish**)

Benjamin Verschoyle (father):

Residence - Marrowbone Lane - August 3, 1796

- Edward Verschoyle & Catherine Verschoyle

  o Elizabeth Verschoyle – b. 30 Mar 1820, bapt. 16 Apr 1820 (Baptism, **St. Luke Parish**)

- Hamilton Verschoyle & Catherine Margaret Verschoyle

  o Sarah Matilda Verschoyle – b. 1838, bapt. 1838 (Baptism, **St. Peter Parish**)

  o Thomasina Verschoyle – b. 16 May 1842, bapt. Jul 1842 (Baptism, **St. Peter Parish**)

  o John Thomas Verschoyle – b. 9 Nov 1846, bapt. 23 Dec 1846 (Baptism, **St. Stephen Parish**)

  o Margaret Emily Verschoyle – b. 12 Apr 1849, bapt. 20 Jun 1849 (Baptism, **St. Peter Parish**)

  o John Thomas Samuel Verschoyle – b. 7 Apr 1851, bapt. 14 May 1851 (Baptism, **St. Peter Parish**)

Hamilton Verschoyle (father):

Residence - Upper Baggot Street - 1838

No 62 Upper Baggot Street - July 1842

December 23, 1846

June 20, 1849

May 14, 1851

Verschoyle Surname Ireland: 1600s to 1900s

Occupation - Clerk in Holy Orders - July 1842

December 23, 1846

June 20, 1849

May 14, 1851

- Henry Verschoyle & Dorothy Unknown, bur. 17 Jul 1799 (Burial, **St. Catherine Parish**)

  o Charles Verschoyle – bapt. 10 Aug 1759 (Baptism, **St. Catherine Parish**)

  o Henry Verschoyle – bapt. 16 Aug 1762 (Baptism, **St. Catherine Parish**)

  o Benjamin Verschoyle – bapt. 11 Sep 1764 (Baptism, **St. Catherine Parish**)

  o William Verschoyle – bapt. 3 May 1768 (Baptism, **St. Catherine Parish**)

Henry Verschoyle (father):

Residence - Marrowbone Lane - September 11, 1764

May 3, 1768

Dorothy Unknown (mother):

Residence - Marrowbone Lane - July 17, 1799

- John Verschoyle, bur. 22 Mar 1801 (Burial, **St. Catherine Parish**) & Elizabeth Unknown, bur. 10 Aug 1806 (Burial, **St. Catherine Parish**)

  o Deborah Verschoyle – bapt. 8 Dec 1776 (Baptism, **St. Catherine Parish**)

  o Elizabeth Verschoyle – bapt. 22 Nov 1778 (Baptism, **St. Catherine Parish**)

John Verschoyle (father):

Residence - Marrowbone Lane - December 8, 1776

November 22, 1768

March 22, 1801

- John Verschoyle & Henrietta Preston – 16 Jul 1782 (Marriage, **St. Audoen Parish**)

  o Joseph Verschoyle – bapt. 29 May 1783 (Baptism, **St. Audoen Parish**)

  o William Verschoyle – bapt. 27 Jan 1786 (Baptism, **St. Audoen Parish**)

Hurst

- John Verschoyle & Mary Ryan – 14 Nov 1841 (Marriage, **St. Catherine Parish** (RC))

  - Catherine Mary Verschoyle & Francis Byrne (B y r n e) – 14 Oct 1867 (Marriage, **Harrington Street Parish** (RC))

    - James Joseph Byrne – b. 3 Jul 1870, bapt. 8 Jul 1870 (Baptism, **St. Nicholas Parish** (RC))

    - William Joseph Byrne – b. 24 Nov 1872, bapt. 29 Nov 1872 (Baptism, **St. Nicholas Parish** (RC))

    - Norah Mary Byrne – b. 25 Apr 1874, bapt. 1 May 1874 (Baptism, **St. Nicholas Parish** (RC))

    - Clare Augusta Byrne – b. 29 Aug 1875, bapt. 2 Sep 1875 (Baptism, **St. Nicholas Parish** (RC))

    - Angelo Ursula Byrne – b. 30 Jul 1877, bapt. 3 Aug 1877 (Baptism, **St. Nicholas Parish** (RC))

Catherine Verschoyle (daughter):

Residence - Unknown

Francis Byrne, son of James Byrne & Jane Smith (son-in-law):

Residence - 22 New Row Street - October 14, 1867

    July 8, 1870

    November 29, 1872

    May 1, 1874

    September 2, 1875

    August 3, 1877

- John Verschoyle & Mary Unknown

  - August Joseph Verschoyle – bapt. 23 Aug 1846 (Baptism, **St. Nicholas Parish** (RC))

- John Verschoyle & Mary Unknown

  - Mary Teresa Verschoyle & John Mayne – 30 Jan 1876 (Marriage, **St. Michan Parish** (RC))

Mary Teresa Verschoyle (daughter):

Residence - 2 East Square Four Courts - January 30, 1876

John Mayne, son of John Mayne & Jane Unknown (son-in-law):

Residence - White Hall-Terrace 2 Circular Road - January 30, 1876

Verschoyle Surname Ireland: 1600s to 1900s

- o Charles Verschoyle & Sarah White – 27 Jul 1879 (Marriage, **St. Nicholas Parish** (RC))

  - ▪ Josephine Verschoyle – b. 7 Oct 1885, bapt. 21 Oct 1885 (Baptism, **St. Mary, Pro Cathedral Parish** (RC))

  - ▪ Augustine Mary Verschoyle – b. 23 May 1887, bapt. 1 Jun 1887 (Baptism, **St. Mary, Pro Cathedral Parish** (RC))

Charles Verschoyle (son):

  Residence - 3 Eglinton Cottages South Circular Road - July 27, 1879

  120 Lower Gloucester Street - October 21, 1885

  Rotunda Hospital - June 1, 1887

Sarah White, daughter of John White & Ellen Unknown (daughter-in-law):

  Residence - 6 Peter Street - July 27, 1879

- • John Verschoyle & Susan Ruth

  - o Richard Verschoyle – bapt. 16 Jul 1827 (Baptism, **St. Nicholas Parish** (RC))

  - o Joseph Verschoyle – bapt. 22 Jul 1834 (Baptism, **St. Nicholas Parish** (RC))

- • John Verschoyle & Unknown

  - o Richard Verschoyle & Emily Edwards – 12 Apr 1853 (Marriage, **St. Anne Parish**)

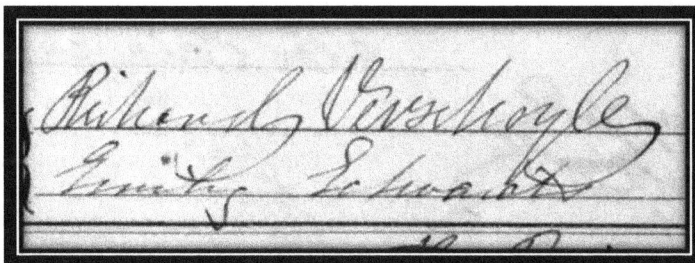

Signatures:

Richard Verschoyle (son):

  Residence - Carlingford - April 12, 1853

  Occupation - CLK (Abbreviation for Clerk)

Emily Edwards, daughter of James K. Edwards (daughter-in-law):

  Residence - 7 Nassau Street - April 12, 1853

Hurst

James K. Edwards (father):

    Occupation - Esquire

John Verschoyle (father):

    Occupation - Esquire

Marriage Witnesses:

Whynerston Edwards

Signature:

- John Hamilton Verschoyle & Florence Lyla Verschoyle

  - Florence Emily Beryl Verschoyle – b. 13 Jul 1885, bapt. 3 Sep 1885 (Baptism, **Richmond Barracks Parish**)

John Hamilton Verschoyle (father):

    Residence - Harcourt Lodge Golden Bridge Dublin - September 3, 1885

    Occupation - Captain D C L I - September 3, 1885

- John James Verschoyle & Catherine Casey – 31 Jan 1853 (Marriage, **St. Nicholas Parish (RC)**)

  - Mary Anne Verschoyle – b. 1 Sep 1856, bapt. 8 Sep 1856 (Baptism, **St. Nicholas Parish (RC)**)

  - Catherine Verschoyle – b. 26 Jun 1858, bapt. 28 Jun 1858 (Baptism, **St. Nicholas Parish (RC)**)

  - John Verschoyle – b. 21 Jan 1861, bapt. Feb 1861 (Baptism, **St. Nicholas Parish (RC)**)

  - Mary Verschoyle, b. 1 Sep 1863, bapt. 11 Sep 1863 (Baptism, **St. Catherine (RC)**) & Thomas Ryan – 22 Aug 1880 (Marriage, **St. Catherine Parish (RC)**)

    - John Christopher Ryan – b. 16 Jan 1881, bapt. 17 Jan 1881 (Baptism, **St. Nicholas Parish (RC)**)

Verschoyle Surname Ireland: 1600s to 1900s

Mary Verschoyle (daughter):

    Residence - 1 Mullinahack Lane - August 22, 1880

Thomas Ryan, son of John Ryan & Jane Unknown (son-in-law):

    Residence - 1 Mullinahack Lane - August 22, 1880

        11 Francis Street - January 17, 1881

John Ryan (father):

    Residence - 12 Plunkett Street - August 22, 1880

    o   Teresa Verschoyle & Patrick Murray – 20 Jul 1884 (Marriage, **St. Mary, Pro Cathedral Parish**

       (RC))

        ▪ John Christopher Murray – b. 15 Mar 1887, bapt. 23 Mar 1887 (Baptism, **St. Mary, Pro**

        Cathedral Parish (RC))

Teresa Verschoyle (daughter):

    Residence - 21 Moore Street - July 20, 1884

Patrick Murray, son of John Murray & Mary Bollard (son-in-law):

    Residence - 10 Norfolk Market - July 20, 1884

        25 Cole's Lane - March 23, 1887

John Verschoyle (father):

    Residence - 7 Kevin Street - September 8, 1856

        7 Mitre Alley - June 28, 1858

        114 Coombe - February 1861

        2 Mullinahack Lane- September 11, 1863

        August 22, 1880

        21 Moore Street - July 20, 1884

Hurst

- John James Verschoyle, b. 1805, d. 6 Aug 1891 (Burial, **Rathcoole Parish**) & Unknown

Signature:

- ○ Helen Catherine Verschoyle & Montray Gledstones – 15 Jan 1874 (Marriage, **Rathcoole Parish**)

Helen Catherine Verschoyle (daughter):

　Residence - Tassagart - January 15, 1874

Montray Gledstones, son of Robert Hornidge Gledstones (son-in-law):

　Residence - Fordross, Clogher, Co. Tyrone - January 15, 1874

　Occupation - SGR - January 15, 1874

Robert Hornidge Gledstones (father):

　Occupation - SGR

- ○ Sarah Wilhelmina Verschoyle & Richard Stewart Dobbs Campbell – 28 Jan 1880 (Marriage, **St. Anne Parish**)

Signatures:

Verschoyle Surname Ireland: 1600s to 1900s

Sarah Wilhelmina Verschoyle (daughter):

>   Residence - 36 Upper Mount Street Dublin - January 28, 1880

Richard Stewart Dobbs Campbell, son of Henry Campbell (son-in-law):

>   Residence - 40 Dawson Street Dublin - January 28, 1880

>   Occupation - Clerk in Holy Orders - January 28, 1880

Henry Campbell (father):

>   Occupation - Gentleman

John James Verschoyle (father):

>   Occupation - Gentleman

Wedding Witnesses:

John James Verschoyle & Margaret Stuart Verschoyle

Signatures:

- o   Catherine Verschoyle & Shuldham Henry Shaw – 25 Oct 1882 (Marriage, **Rathcoole Parish**)

Catherine Verschoyle (daughter):

>   Residence - Tassaggart - October 25, 1882

Shuldham Henry Shaw, son of Joseph Shaw (son-in-law):

>   Residence - Tassaggart, Saggart - October 25, 1882

>   Occupation - Sergeant - October 25, 1882

Joseph Shaw (father):

>   Occupation - Sergeant

Hurst

o   Margaret Stuart Verschoyle & Duncan Brownlow – 28 Mar 1883 (Marriage, **Rathcoole Parish**)

Signature:

Margaret Stuart Verschoyle (daughter):

   Residence - Tassaggart - March 28, 1883

Duncan Brownlow, son of John Brownlow (son-in-law):

   Residence - An Bracan, Rectory, Navan - March 28, 1883

   Occupation - Clerk - March 28, 1883

John Brownlow (father):

   Occupation - Clerk Dean

John James Verschoyle (father):

   Residence - Tassaggart, Saggart Co. Dublin - August 6, 1891

   Occupation - Sergeant

                     Gentleman

                     Sergeant D

Age at Death - 86 years

Verschoyle Surname Ireland: 1600s to 1900s

- Joseph Verschoyle & Unknown

  - James Lorenzo Verschoyle & Caroline Elizabeth Comtesse D'Assereto – 24 Feb 1868 (Marriage, **St. Peter Parish**)

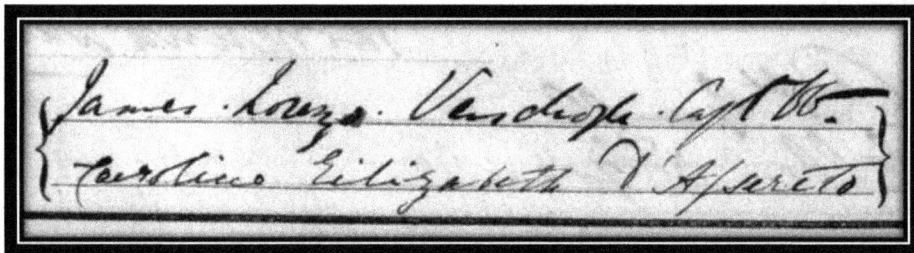

Signatures:

   - George Mautray Verschoyle – b. 15 Mar 1875, bapt. 2 May 1875 (Baptism, **Taney Parish**)

Joseph Lorenzo Verschoyle (son):

   Residence - Fitzwilliam Square - February 24, 1868

      Roebuck Hill - May 2, 1875

   Occupation - Captain in 66th Regiment - February 24, 1868

      Gentleman - May 2, 1875

Caroline Elizabeth Comtesse D'Assereto, daughter of Louis Charles Marquis D'Assereto (daughter-in-law):

   Residence - Tarpey's Hotel Nallan Street - February 24, 1868

Louis Charles Marquis D'Assereto (father):

   Occupation - Marquis D'Assereto

Joseph Verschoyle (father):

   Occupation - Clerk in Holy Orders

Hurst

- Robert Verschoyle & Margaret Bill – 2 Sep 1680 (Marriage, **St. Catherine Parish**)

- Robert Verschoyle & Martha Verschoyle

  o Robert Verschoyle – bapt. 29 Oct 1725 (Baptism, **St. Catherine Parish**)

- Robert Verschoyle & Mary Verschoyle

  o George Thomas Verschoyle – bapt. 3 May 1761 (Baptism, **St. Mark Parish**)

Robert Verschoyle (father):

 Residence - George's Quay - May 3, 1761

- Robert Henry Verschoyle & Gertrude Mary Verschoyle

  o Catherine Mildred Verschoyle – b. 6 Dec 1873, bapt. 8 Jan 1874 (Baptism, **Leeson Park Parish**)

Robert Henry Verschoyle (father):

 Residence - 19 Fitzwilliam Square - January 8, 1874

 Occupation - Major H P H M S

- Thomas Verschoyle & Elizabeth Verschoyle

  o Richard Verschoyle – bapt. 12 Nov 1739 (Baptism, **St. Catherine Parish**)

- Unknown Verschoyle & Unknown

  o Joseph Verschoyle & Catherine Jephson – 3 Jul 1827 (Marriage, **St. Peter Parish**)

Joseph Verschoyle (son):

 Residence - Killala Castle, Co. Mayo - July 3, 1827

 Occupation - Reverend - July 3, 1827

Catherine Jephson, daughter of Unknown Jephson (daughter-in-law):

 Residence - Merrion Square - July 3, 1827

Verschoyle Surname Ireland: 1600s to 1900s

- Unknown Verschoyle & Unknown

  - Richard Verschoyle & Margaret Davenport Lloyd – 19 Jul 1841 (Marriage, **St. Peter Parish**)

Richard Verschoyle (son):

    Residence - Loughally, Armagh - July 19, 1841

    Occupation - Clerk (Reverend) - July 19, 1841

Margaret Davenport Lloyd, daughter of Unknown Davenport Lloyd (daughter-in-law):

    Residence - Leeson Street - July 19, 1841

    Occupation - Spinster - July 19, 1841

  - Matilda Mary Verschoyle & Rawdan Griffith Greene – 10 May 1844 (Marriage, **St. Peter Parish**)

Mary Matilda Verschoyle (daughter):

    Residence - 36 Upper Mount Street - May 10, 1844

    Occupation - Spinster - May 10, 1844

Rawdan Griffith Greene, son of Unknown Greene (son-in-law):

    Residence - Sandaler, Co. Kent - May 10, 1844

    Occupation - Reverend, Clerk - May 10, 1844

- William Verschoyle & Anne Verschoyle

  - Anne Verschoyle – b. 1797, bapt. 31 Aug 1797 (Baptism, **St. James Parish**)

- William Verschoyle & Sarah Bryan

  - Susan Christine Verschoyle – b. 26 Dec 1859, bapt. 22 Jan 1860 (Baptism, **St. Nicholas Parish** (RC))

William Verschoyle (The father):

    Residence - Ropers Rest - January 22, 1860

- William Henry Foster Verschoyle & H. H. Frances

Signature:

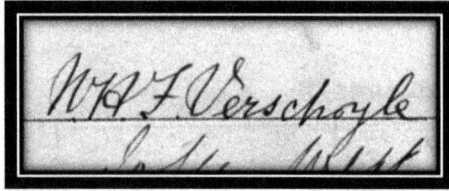

- o   Kathleen Laura Verschoyle – b. 7 Jul 1892, bapt. 27 Jul 1892 (Baptism, **Taney Parish**)

- o   Francis Stuart Verschoyle – b. 9 Apr 1896, bapt. 30 May 1896 (Baptism, **Taney Parish**)

William Henry Foster Verschoyle (father):

Residence - Wardley - July 27, 1892

Woodly Dundrum - May 30, 1896

Occupation - Esquire - July 27, 1892

Land Agent - May 30, 1896

Individual Births/Baptisms

None were Listed

Individual Burials

- Charles Verschoyle – bur. 26 Aug 1760 (Burial, **St. Catherine Parish**)

- George Verschoyle – bur. 26 May 1725 (Burial, **St. Catherine Parish**)

George Verschoyle (deceased):

> **Age at Death - child**

- George Verschoyle – bur. 29 Nov 1728 (Burial, **St. Catherine Parish**)

George Verschoyle (deceased):

> **Age at Death - child**

- Henry Verschoyle – bur. 10 Jul 1722 (Burial, **St. Catherine Parish**)

- Henry Verschoyle – bur. 17 Feb 1804 (Burial, **St. Catherine Parish**)

Henry Verschoyle (deceased):

> **Residence - Robert Street - Before February 17, 1804**

- Henry Verschoyle – bur. 5 Jun 1734 (Burial, **St. Catherine Parish**)

- James Verschoyle – bur. 2 Dec 1788 (Burial, **St. Paul Parish**)

- James Verschoyle – bur. 28 Nov 1811 (Burial, **St. Werburgh Parish**)

James Verschoyle (deceased):

> **Residence - Castle Street - Before November 28, 1811**
>
> **Cause of Death - sudden death**

- John Verschoyle – bur. 26 Aug 1729 (Burial, **St. Catherine Parish**)

- Joseph Verschoyle – bur. 17 Apr 1796 (Burial, **St. Catherine Parish**)

Joseph Harris (deceased):

> **Residence - Cork Street - Before April 17, 1796**
>
> **Occupation - Esquire - April 17, 1796**

Verschoyle Surname Ireland: 1600s to 1900s

- Joseph Verschoyle – bur. 24 Jul 1810 (Burial, **St. Catherine Parish**)

- Margaret Verschoyle – bur. 9 Dec 1773 (Burial, **St. Catherine Parish**)

- Richard Verschoyle – bur. 18 Jan 1828 (Burial, **St. Catherine Parish**)

- Richard Jephson Verschoyle – b. Nov 1837, d. 22 Apr 1857, bur. 24 Apr 1857 (Burial, **Arbour Hill Barracks Parish**)

Richard Jephson Verschoyle (deceased):

  Occupation - Ensign 3rd Battalion's 60 Rifles

  Age at Death - 19 years 6 months

  Cause of Death - phlegmonous

- Unknown Verschoyle – bur. 15 Mar 1787 (Burial, **St. Paul Parish**)

- William Verschoyle – bur. 9 Feb 1757 (Burial, **St. Catherine Parish**)

- William Verschoyle – bur. 27 Nov 1785 (Burial, **St. Catherine Parish**)

William Verschoyle (deceased):

  Residence - Bride Street - Before November 27, 1785

Individual Marriages

- Anne Verschoyle & Patrick Rooney

  o Susan Rooney – bapt. 21 Feb 1841 (Baptism, **St. James Parish** (RC))

- Catherine Verschoyle & Thomas Kennedy

  o Anne Kennedy & Bernard (B e r n a r d) Heyburn – 8 Aug 1886 (Marriage, **St. Mary, Pro Cathedral Parish** (RC))

Anne Kennedy (daughter):

Residence - **5 Moore Street** - August 8, 1886

Bernard Heyburn, son of James Heyburn & Catherine Graves (son-in-law):

Residence - **6 Corn Market** - August 8, 1886

- Elizabeth Verschoyle & James Bond

  o Esther Bond – bapt. 15 Mar 1847 (Baptism, **St. Nicholas Parish** (RC))

  o Thomas Bond – bapt. 6 Aug 1852 (Baptism, **St. Nicholas Parish** (RC))

- Elizabeth Verschoyle & Patrick Hoey

  o Anne Hoey & John Mulligan – 26 Feb 1865 (Marriage, **St. Catherine Parish** (RC))

Anne Hoey (daughter):

Residence - **74 Marrowbone Lane** - February 26, 1865

John Mulligan, son of James Mulligan & Catherine Weydock (son-in-law):

Residence - **74 Marrowbone Lane** - February 26, 1865

Verschoyle Surname Ireland: 1600s to 1900s

- Julia Verschoyle & Terence Reilly – 11 Sep 1855 (Marriage, **St. Nicholas Parish (RC)**)

  o John William Reilly – b. 23 Jun 1856, bapt. 9 Jul 1856 (Baptism, **St. Mary, Pro Cathedral Parish (RC)**)

Terence Reilly (father):

   Residence - 21 Great Mecklenburgh Street - July 9, 1856

- Mary Verschoyle & Bernard (B e r n a r d) Barry (B a r r y) – 5 Aug 1850 (Marriage, **St. Nicholas Parish (RC)**)

  o Julia Barry – b. 28 Nov 1862, bapt. 10 Dec 1862 (Baptism, **St. Nicholas Parish (RC)**)

Bernard Barry (father):

   Residence - 36 Coombe - December 10, 1862

Name Variations

Includes Latin and Abbreviated forms of names found in the original documents.

Anne = Ann, Anna, Annae, Annie

Benjamin = Benjn

Catherine = Cath, Cathe, Cathne, Catharin, Catharina, Catharinae, Catharinam, Catharine, Catherin, Catherinae, Catherinam, Kate, Kathrine, Katharine, Katherine

Charles = Chas

Christine = Christina

Dorothy = Doraty

Edward = Edwardus, Edwd

Eleanor = Eleonor, Elianor, Elinor, Elnr, Ellnor, Nellie, Nora

Elizabeth = Eliz, Eliza, Elizabet, Elizth, Bessie

Frances = Frans

Francis = Fran

George = Geo, Georg

Henry = Henery, Henricus

James = Jacobi, Jacobum, Jacobus, Jas

Jane = Joanna, Joanne

John = Jno, Joannes, Joannis

Joseph = Jos, Josh

Josephine = Josephina

Margaret = Margartia, Margeret, Margarett, Margeret, Magerett, Margret, Mgt, Margt, Margtt

Mary = Maria, Mariae, Mariam

Verschoyle Surname Ireland: 1600s to 1900s

Mary Anne = Mary Ann, Maryann, Maryanne, Marian, Mariane, Mariann, Mariannae, Marianne

Matthew = Mat, Matt, Mathew

Michael = Michaelis, Mich, Miche, Michl, Michll

Patrick = Pat, Patt, Patk, Patricii

Richard = Richd

Robert = Robt

Teresa = Theresa

Thomas = Thos, Ths

William = Willm, Wm

Notes

Notes

Notes

Notes

Notes

Notes

Index

Edward
1799 Sep 22.. 1
Elizabeth
1778 Nov 22.. 3
1820 Apr 16 2
Florence Emily Beryl
1885 Sep 3.. 6
Francis Stuart
1896 May 30 14
George Mautray
1875 May 2 11
George Thomas
1761 May 3 12
Henry
1762 Aug 16 3
James
1870 Jul 8 1
Jane
1861 Sep 9.. 1
John
1861 Feb 6
John Thomas
1846 Dec 23 2
John Thomas Samuel
1851 May 14 2
Joseph
1783 May 29 3
1834 Jul 22 5
Josephine
1885 Oct 21.. 5
Josephine Mary
1877 Oct 11.. 1
Kathleen Laura
1892 Jul 27 14
Margaret Emily
1849 Jun 20.. 2
Mary
1796 Aug 3 2
1858 Aug 16 1
1863 Sep 11 6
Mary Anne
1856 Sep 8.. 6
Richard
1739 Nov 12 12

1827 Jul 16.. 5
Robert
1725 Oct 29.. 12
Sarah Matilda
1838 2
Susan Christine
1860 Jan 22.. 13
Susanna Bridget Josephine
1857 Jan 1.. 1
Thomas Patrick
1860 Mar 3.. 1
Thomasina
1842 Jul 2
William
1768 May 3 3
1786 Jan 27 3

Births
Anne
1797 13
Anne Virginia Frances
1872 Sep 8.. 1
Augustine Mary
1887 May 23 5
Catherine
1858 Jun 26.. 6
Catherine Mildred
1873 Dec 6 12
Elizabeth
1820 Mar 30.. 2
Florence Emily Beryl
1885 Jul 13.. 6
Francis Stuart
1896 Apr 9 14
George Mautray
1875 Mar 15.. 11
James
1870 Jul 6 1
Jane
1861 Aug 28 1
John
1861 Jan 21.. 6
John James
1805 8
John Thomas

About The Author

Donovan Hurst graduated from San Diego State University with a Bachelor of Arts in the major field of studies of History and a minor in the field of studies of Anthropology. He is a current member of The General Society of Mayflower Descendants and has been conducting genealogical research for over 10 years tracing back his ancestors to their ancestral homelands in Denmark, England, France, Germany, Ireland, Norway, and Scotland.

www.ingramcontent.com/pod-product-compliance
Lightning Source LLC
Chambersburg PA
CBHW081205270326
41930CB00014B/3302